BEYOND THE STRAIGHT PATH

MY REFLECTION IN DISSONANC

Ashney Harryton

BEYOND THE STRAIGHT PATH
MY REFLECTION IN DISSONANCE

By Ashney Harryton
Polishing Company Book Writing League

Library of Congress Control Number (LCCN): 2024952480

ISBN (Hardcover): 978-1-965408-48-3

ISBN (Ebook): 9781965408506

ISBN (Paperback): 978-1-965408-47-6

Contact Information:
Ashney Harryton
Aharryton@yahoo.com

Dedication

This book is dedicated to my family, with a mix of gratitude and reluctance, for urging me to write this memoir and for their unwavering support through every step of my journey.

A special thank you to Whitney, Jay, and JC, whose sleepless nights were spent in concern for my well-being when I struggled to care for myself. Your love and care have been a guiding light in the darkest times.

Table of Contents

BEYOND THE STRAIGHT PATH

In August 2024, I set off on a journey that would forever change my perspective on the world, traveling to Japan and Seoul, Korea, from August 16 to August 30. As I stepped into these vibrant cities, I was immediately captivated by their distinct cultures, yet there was an undeniable thread connecting them—a deep-rooted beauty, a profound respect for tradition, and a culinary scene that tantalized my senses. Each moment felt like a discovery, filled with awe and wonder, as I immersed myself in the rich history and the warm hospitality that enveloped me. From the tranquil temples of Kyoto to the bustling streets of Seoul, this adventure was not just a trip; it was a heartfelt experience that ignited my passion for exploration and left an indelible mark on my soul.

Japan

Japan was an experience that surpassed my highest expectations. Known for its rich cultural heritage and mesmerizing landscapes, Japan's charm lies in its balance of tradition and modernity. From the bustling streets of Tokyo to the serene temples of Kyoto, every corner was a scene to beauty and precision. The cleanliness of the cities was impeccable, and the respect ingrained in the people's interactions was truly inspiring. And the food—whether it was fresh sushi, warm bowls of ramen, or delicate matcha desserts—was a sensory delight that I'll never forget.

Seoul, Korea

Seoul, Korea, was equally captivating, particularly for its emphasis on self-care and beauty. Korea's skincare industry is renowned for its innovation, with a culture deeply invested in beauty regimens that include facial fillers, Botox, and other treatments aimed at preserving youthful appearances. Beyond skincare, Seoul's fashion scene was cutting-edge, and the food was nothing short of extraordinary. Korean soul food was a revelation, offering flavors that were comforting yet bold, while the famous Korean BBQ was an unforgettable experience, with rich flavors and succulent meats that were simply out of this world.

This trip was a journey through beauty, respect, and unforgettable flavors, leaving a lasting impression on my heart and soul.

Upon my return to the U.S. on August 30, 2024, what I thought would be a simple re-entry turned into a life-altering ordeal. At JFK Airport, instead of a warm welcome, I was met with handcuffs and confusion. I was informed that there was a fugitive warrant out for my arrest from another state. My mind raced—I had no criminal record, no prior arrests, and certainly no idea of any warrant.

It all stemmed from a house purchase back in May, where I put a down payment of $30,000 on a house Not a car. However, the property had couple of Antique shelves of cars that was left by the previous owner.

Keep reading you will be shock to hear my so- called crimes. What began as a civil dispute had somehow escalated into a criminal case, completely unbeknownst to me. As Port Authority officers questioned me, I tried to make sense of it all. I was told I "Fit the color," whatever that meant, as if my appearance alone was enough to justify my detention.

One of the officers, a Ukrainian man with a surprisingly good sense of humor, tried to lighten the mood by offering me a donut and some water after I'd been detained for 14 hours. I appreciated the gesture, but the situation was far from humorous. I thought the nightmare would end once I was transported to court, but it only got worse. The fugitive warrant held firm, and to my disbelief, I was denied bail.

I was given a court date of September 9, 2024, at 9:30 AM, but deep down, I knew that would likely be delayed. For now, I had no choice but to head back to my jail cell and face this new reality.

On August 31, 2024, I found myself at the infamous Rikers Island, a place notorious for its harsh conditions and unsettling reputation. Temporary processing began around 7 PM, and for the first two hours, I was isolated, left to reflect on how drastically my life had shifted in just a few days. Soon, another detainee—a woman clearly strung out on drugs—was brought in, just as they served dinner. The meal? Two slices of dry wheat bread, soggy canned green beans, limp carrots, and an apple. I passed on the meal, but my new companion was all too eager to dig in.

Regrettably, that cup of water I'd accepted earlier at JFK was something I soon came to regret. The intake bathroom was a nightmare—feces piled high in the toilet, which refused to flush. The only source of water came from a tiny faucet attached to the toilet, a situation so unsanitary that I decided dehydration was the safer option. For four days, I didn't drink a drop of water, forcing myself to endure until they finally handed me a medicine cup-sized portion of water.

Survival in Rikers was a mental battle from the start. Every minute felt like an eternity, and the brutal reality of my situation was impossible to escape. From the appalling hygiene to the shocking food, my arrival on Rikers Island was a stark reminder that I had entered a world far removed from anything I had ever known.

On Tuesday, September 3, 2024, something unexpected happened. Amid the chaos of Rikers Island, where everything felt out of control, I experienced a small but significant moment. My name was called, and for the first time in my life, someone pronounced it correctly on the first try.

It may seem like a minor detail, but for me, it was deeply meaningful. I'm used to hearing Americans break my name into strange, awkward syllables, as if it were a puzzle they couldn't quite solve. They do it to names like "Barbara" too, saying "Bar-Bara" with a staccato rhythm that never quite feels right. But this time, it flowed naturally, without hesitation or missteps.

In a place where my identity felt stripped away, where I was reduced to a number in the system, this simple act—hearing my name spoken correctly—felt like a small but powerful reminder of who I was. It stuck with me, a quiet moment of dignity in an otherwise undignified environment.

After what felt like an eternity, booking intake was finally over, and I was about to face the real experience of jail. The process began with the transport to my cell—the clanging of keys, the crackling radios, and the tense presence of other inmates along the way. The walk to my destination felt like a journey into the unknown, each step heavier than the last.

Before reaching the actual cell, I encountered the most humiliating part of the entire ordeal. A female officer stood before me and ordered me to undress completely. As if that wasn't degrading enough, three male officers sat nearby, watching through a camera. There was no privacy, no dignity left to hold onto. Piece by piece, I stripped away my clothes—pants, shirt, bra, underwear, shoes, socks— until I stood there, utterly exposed.

The pat-down followed, as multiple hands moved over my body, searching for weapons. The absurdity of it all struck me, and in a desperate attempt to cope, I found a moment of humor. I laughed silently at the thought of hiding a handgun—knowing full well how impossible that would be. I had come straight from JFK International Airport, after all, where even carrying toothpaste had been out of the question in Japan, let alone something dangerous.

That brief, bitter laugh was the only relief I had in that moment of vulnerability. It was a cruel reminder of the complete loss of control and humanity I was now enduring, one strip at a time.

After the invasive pat-down, the next step was just as dehumanizing. The officers instructed me to lift my breasts so they could check underneath, but I couldn't comply— three years ago, I had a breast lift, and they didn't move the way they expected. I explained, but they moved on quickly, asking me to turn around so they could check my back. They were looking for anything hidden along my spine, but of course, there was nothing to find.

Then, from the "bubble"—the surveillance room—a male officer's voice boomed, instructing the female officer to make me squat and cough. I was ordered to squat down, spread my buttocks with both hands, and cough three times. It felt like I was being stripped of my last shred of dignity. Afterward, I was told to turn around and face the officers again. The male voice came over the intercom once more, commanding me to squat again, this time to open my vaginal lips and cough three more times. In that moment, I felt less than human. Worse than a dog. I couldn't believe this was happening to me. I questioned everything—my life, my existence, and how I ended up here.

With sarcasm as my only defense, I turned to the female officer and said, "I hope you like what you see." Her response was cold and indifferent: "I'm just doing my job."

By then, exhaustion had settled deep into my bones. I was hungry, thirsty, filthy, and smelled awful. I had reached a point where I would have confessed to anything, just to make it stop—even though I hadn't even gotten a parking ticket in my life. The silence that followed was punctuated by the sound of keys rattling and doors slamming, loud enough to jolt anyone from a stupor. It was the harsh reality of jail, and it hit me full force.

When I was escorted to the 4th South dormitory at Rikers Island, I quickly realized that jail was nothing like what I'd imagined. The officer leading the way—a woman whose name and ID badge were deliberately hidden—held a set of heavy keys that jingled constantly as we walked. Accompanying her were two male officers, ready to take me to my dorm. This wasn't the typical dormitory setup; it housed 40 inmates, a mix of both men and women. I was stunned to learn that men and women lived together in the same space.

When I arrived at my bed, I immediately noticed two men nearby—one stationed at the foot of my bed, the other just two beds down. This was completely foreign to me. I had never lived with men I wasn't related to, let alone in a jail setting. Having never been arrested or spent time in jail before, it all felt surreal.

One of the first things I asked the officers was, "Is there any way I can keep my debit card?" They burst out laughing and asked, "Ma'am, for what?" I innocently replied, "To buy something from the vending machine." That's when an older male inmate, who had been quietly observing, interjected, "Mommy, there are no vending machines here. Only your 'books.'" At that moment, I didn't understand what he meant, but I soon learned that "books" referred to the jail's internal currency system—far from the conveniences of the outside world I was used to.

This was a new reality—one where even the simplest assumptions no longer applied, and the rules were dictated by the walls around me.

It didn't take long for everyone to recognize me as the "new inmate," or the "first-timer," as they all called me. The realization hit hard—if tears alone could unlock the gates of Rikers Island, I would have been long gone. I stood there with a plastic bag in hand, feeling out of place and overwhelmed. Inside the bag was my new reality: a thin mat that would serve as my bed, an extra pair of brown pants, and a shirt, both marked as 2X. I normally wore a medium, but the officers had made that decision for me without asking.

Oddly enough, I didn't mind the oversized clothes. On Rikers, where appearances meant little and vulnerability could be dangerous, being less noticeable felt like a hidden blessing. Blending in seemed like the safest option in an environment where standing out could attract the wrong kind of attention.

From my bed on the 4th South dormitory, I had an unexpected view—one that felt like a cruel reminder of what I was missing. In the distance, I could see the ocean glistening, the iconic Brooklyn and Manhattan Bridges, and, just beyond them, the Rikers Bridge. That bridge was the only way off this island, a tantalizing sight, yet completely out of reach.

Each day, the reality of my situation set in a little more. The bridge, the city skyline, the freedom I had taken for granted—they all seemed impossibly far away, a constant reminder of the life I once had, now suspended in limbo on this island of despair.

Chaos on the Phone

Just then, the chaos escalated. I heard the unmistakable slam of a phone followed by a piercing scream: "Stupid white bitch!" My eyes darted up, and there was Malik, fully immersed in yet another eruption of anger. He turned to me, asking if I had a call. Of course, I didn't. The phone had become a coveted lifeline in this place, and I had long since given up hope of connecting with anyone outside these walls.

Malik didn't wait for my answer. He snatched the phone, his voice booming as he yelled into the receiver, "You listening now, stupid white bitch?" It was a familiar scene, one I had witnessed before, the way he would lash out with crude insults as if they were second nature. But then, almost as if someone had flicked a switch, he calmed down. His tone shifted dramatically, transforming from one of aggression to something softer, almost respectful. "Beloved," he said, "you're an unfinished product."

His words caught me off guard. I leaned in, intrigued by the sudden change. Malik continued, explaining that he considered himself unfinished—not just in life, but in his transition. He had undergone hormone treatments and surgery to remove his breasts, but the final piece of the puzzle was still missing: the full implant that would complete his transition. Until that happened, he felt like he was caught in a limbo, existing in a world that struggled to see him for who he truly was.

In his mind, Malik was already "he," despite what society might still perceive. This idea of being "unfinished" resonated deeply with me, especially in this environment where so many of us felt like fragments of our true selves. It made me think about the complexity of identity, how it can be shaped by society's expectations and personal experiences.

As he spoke, I could see the vulnerability lurking beneath his tough exterior. Malik was wrestling with more than just his physical transition; he was navigating the choppy waters of acceptance—both self-acceptance and societal acceptance. His anger often masked a profound sadness, a frustration at being perceived as something he wasn't. In a place where labels were handed out freely, Malik was striving to redefine his identity on his own terms, even if the world around him wasn't ready to embrace that change.

In that moment, as I listened to Malik speak with a surprising tenderness about his journey, I felt a strange kinship with him. We were all unfinished products in our own right, each grappling with our circumstances, trying to make sense of our identities in a space that often felt suffocating. Malik's story reminded me that despite the chaos around us, there was still room for growth, for understanding, and perhaps, for healing. As he hung up the phone, I wondered how many of us would ever feel complete, truly seen, or understood within these walls.

Understanding the Alphabet Community

Being here at Rikers has opened my eyes to the complexities of the "alphabet community." I use that term out of respect, wanting to be inclusive of everyone who identifies with a letter I might not know. The last time I checked, it was LGBTQ+, but if I've missed any letters or nuances, I sincerely apologize. My understanding of this community is limited, and this environment has shown me just how little I know about certain subjects, especially when it comes to identities and experiences outside my own.

In a place like this, where labels are often thrown around haphazardly, it's refreshing to see how people identify and support each other, regardless of the challenges they face. I've met individuals who embody the spirit of their respective identities, each one carrying their stories like badges of honor. Their courage to live authentically, even within the confines of a place like Rikers, has been both enlightening and inspiring.

Our favorite Chef was on the phone again, his voice rising above the din of the dormitory. After hanging up, he muttered, "That bitch is tripping," referring to someone who wasn't complying with demands. In this context, "tripping" means not following the rules, and it's a common term around here. For some reason, the Chef seemed to take a liking to me. Maybe it was because his parents were from the same country as mine, creating a sense of camaraderie.

This connection gave me a few advantages, like getting a cup of water or making a phone call without someone hanging up on me—small but significant gestures of kindness in this harsh environment.

I call him our favorite Chef not because of his culinary skills—though he does a commendable job with the limited resources—but because he's the one serving us our meals. He carries the weight of responsibility on his shoulders, trying to keep things running smoothly amidst the chaos. After another tense phone call with his public defender, he let out a long sigh and said, "They're going to indict me."

At that moment, I leaned in closer, my interest piqued. I felt like a child in kindergarten, eager for story time, ready to absorb every word. The gravity of his situation hung in the air, and I could sense the fear behind his bravado. He was facing the prospect of legal troubles that could deepen his already precarious circumstances.

In this environment, where everyone is grappling with their own challenges, the Chef's admission struck a chord with me. It reminded me that beneath the surface of each person here lies a complex story, filled with struggles and aspirations. As I listened intently, I realized that understanding the alphabet community—or anyone, for that matter—requires more than just knowing the labels; it demands empathy and a willingness to listen to the narratives behind those identities.

This connection, albeit fragile, allowed me to see the humanity in those around me, even when it felt like the world was trying to strip it away. In moments like these, when someone opened up, I felt a flicker of hope that perhaps, in this chaotic place, we could find understanding and support amid the turmoil.

Cultural Reflection

As I sat there, reflecting on my conversation with the Chef, I couldn't help but ponder how much people change when they move to America. It's as if they trade their cultural values, ethics, and morals for the elusive American dream. The pressure to fit in, to succeed, and to assimilate can be overwhelming, and I've fallen victim to that bias myself. I often catch myself questioning whether the compromises I've made have been worth it.

In this harsh environment, where survival often overshadows personal growth, I watched others grapple with similar dilemmas. Each individual I encountered carried their own narrative of adaptation, some clinging tightly to their roots while others seemed to shed their identities like old skin. The duality of maintaining one's culture while striving for acceptance in a new world was a constant theme, one that echoed in the conversations around me.

Lost in my thoughts, I barely noticed Mr. Malik approaching. With his hands casually tucked into his pants, he stood beside me and asked, "You don't know why Sullivan's here, do you?" When I admitted that I didn't, he smirked, a knowing glint in his eyes.

"Let me enlighten you," Malik said, leaning in conspiratorially. He explained that Sullivan—our favorite Chef—had ended up in Rikers because he and a co-defendant had attempted to rob a small Arab-owned store at gunpoint. I listened, intrigued and horrified, as Malik recounted the details. Apparently, Sullivan had pointed the gun at the store owner's head and pulled the trigger, only to find that the gun had jammed.

Malik laughed, shaking his head in disbelief. "What an idiot," he scoffed. "He didn't even wear a ski mask! Who goes into a robbery without one?" His tone was mocking, but there was an edge of sincerity in his disbelief.

I had so many questions swirling in my mind—Did you wear a mask during your crime? Are you smarter now?—but I couldn't bring myself to ask. Instead, I sat quietly, absorbing the reality of the situation. The irony wasn't lost on me; here we were, in a place meant for rehabilitation, and yet the stories shared often reinforced the very cycles we were trapped in.

As I contemplated Sullivan's choices, I wondered about the cultural implications behind his actions. Had he felt pressured to prove himself in this new world, leading him down a path of desperation? Or was it a reflection of deeper societal issues that often left people feeling marginalized and powerless?

In this space, I realized that understanding the complexities of each person's journey meant recognizing the multitude of factors that shaped their decisions. It forced me to confront my own assumptions and biases about identity and morality, especially in a country where dreams and realities often collide in chaotic ways. Here in Rikers, the stories weren't just about crime and punishment; they were about the very human experience of trying to navigate a world that often felt unwelcoming.

Sullivan's Crime

Now I understood the gravity of Sullivan's situation. He wasn't just in here for a petty crime; he was facing an attempted murder charge. Sullivan had a naïve confidence that the charges would be dropped, but I couldn't help but wonder why on earth the district attorney would ever consider dropping an attempted murder charge. It was a serious accusation, and Sullivan's lack of remorse made it even more troubling. In fact, he had the audacity to say, "I should have pistol-whipped that n***er. He's lucky." His arrogance baffled me, revealing a mindset that seemed unrepentant and detached from the severity of his actions.

What really struck me was the casual way he discussed his crime. Sullivan had mentioned that not wearing a mask was his biggest mistake, as if that was the sole error in his thought process during the robbery. Another inmate, Lowe, chimed in with a question about the kind of gun Sullivan had used. "A .45 semi-automatic," Sullivan replied, shrugging as if discussing the weather. "It was old—belonged to my beater mom."

Lowe raised an eyebrow, skepticism written all over his face. "Are you sure she wasn't setting you up?" he asked, but Sullivan brushed it off with a wave of his hand, saying that his dad was his co-defendant, as if that absolved him of any suspicion.

As Sullivan continued to rattle on about his case, I couldn't help but feel a mix of disbelief and concern. He seemed almost proud of the chaos he had caused. "If the surveillance camera caught me, I'm going to trial," he said nonchalantly, "because my lawyer warned me I could face 25 years to life." It was as if he was discussing a game plan for a sports match, not the reality of potentially spending the rest of his life behind bars.

Frustrated by the situation, Sullivan picked up the phone to call his mother. I watched as he explained the circumstances to her, his tone shifting from bravado to desperation. Apparently, she was on her way to visit him at Rikers, and I could see the hope flicker in his eyes at the thought of her support. But a deeper part of me wondered if that support would even matter in the grand scheme of things.

The stark contrast between Sullivan's attitude and the reality of his situation weighed heavily on my mind. In this world where survival often meant adapting to the harshest of circumstances, Sullivan's bravado felt out of place. He was surrounded by individuals whose lives had been shattered by choices that mirrored his, yet he seemed blissfully unaware of the risks he had taken. I felt a sense of foreboding, knowing that arrogance rarely protects one from the consequences of their actions. In this place, that lesson was often learned the hard way.

As I listened to Sullivan's conversation, I couldn't help but reflect on the larger narrative at play. Here we were, trapped in a system that often failed to recognize the humanity in each of us, and yet Sullivan seemed to revel in his perceived power. I realized that understanding his story—and the stories of those around me—was essential in navigating the complexities of this harsh environment. It was a sobering reminder that while we all share a common struggle; our individual paths could lead us to vastly different destinies.

Family Ties to Rikers

While Sullivan continued his conversation on the phone, his tone shifted as he chatted with his sister, attempting to calm himself down before speaking with his "bitch." It was a stark reminder of the complicated dynamics at play within these walls. I watched as Sullivan smirked, a self-satisfied glint in his eyes, and I couldn't help but feel a pang of sympathy for the young woman on the other end of the line.

Africa, another inmate nearby, overheard their conversation and leaned in with curiosity. "How can your mom come visit so easily?" she asked, her voice tinged with disbelief. Sullivan's smirk widened as he replied, "My mom knows everything about Rikers. She served time here, too. My little sister was even born here."

Africa's eyes widened in shock. "Oh shit," she muttered, shaking her head. "That's exactly what I'm trying to avoid for my kids. I don't want them to think it's okay to be here." Her words hung in the air, heavy with the weight of lived experience. It was clear she had a fierce determination to break the cycle that seemed to ensnare so many families.

The revelation of Sullivan's family ties to Rikers painted a vivid picture of generational struggles. His casual mention of his mother's history felt like a badge of honor to him, but for Africa, it was a cautionary tale. She was determined to create a different narrative for her children, one that didn't include the stark reality of prison life. In her eyes, the normalization of incarceration was a battle she had to fight with every ounce of her being.

As I sat there, I reflected on how easy it was for the younger generation to find themselves caught in a system that seemed predestined for failure. Sullivan's flippant attitude toward his family's history was a stark contrast to

Africa's resolve. I could sense her fear and desperation to shield her children from the very environment she had found herself in. The echo of her voice lingered in my mind, reminding me that the chains of the past often tried to ensnare the future.

The conversation turned my thoughts inward, challenging my understanding of the ties that bind us to our families. The idea that a mother could visit her son in prison, having once called it home herself, was a concept I struggled to grasp. How did that shape their relationships? What did it mean to have family ties to a place like Rikers?

In this complex web of connections, each story unfolded layers of pain, resilience, and hope. Sullivan's flippancy clashed sharply with Africa's determination, and I wondered what the future held for those trapped within these walls. Would they break the cycle, or would they find themselves repeating the same mistakes? The journey through this prison was not just about survival; it was about redefining the narratives we carried and the futures we aspired to create.

Rumblings in Rikers

Africa kept rumbling on, "Shit, yes, I said that!" Her words echoed through the dimly lit dormitory, a blend of laughter and anger intermingling in the air. The constant foul language felt like a lifeline in a place where expressing oneself often came down to raw, unfiltered emotion. It struck me how, in here, it seemed like the only way we could demand attention or assert our existence.

She finally turned her gaze to me, curiosity flickering in her eyes. "Why are you here among us? You don't look like someone who's committed a crime or used drugs." I felt the weight of her question, the keen interest not just stemming from nosiness, but from a deeper need to understand the stories we all carried. "So, what did you do?" she pressed.

I listened carefully, remembering the old proverb: "A dog who carries a bone also brings a bone." With that in mind, I exercised my silence, gauging the atmosphere around me. This seemed to frustrate her, and I could see the gears turning in her mind as she tried to draw me out.

"Did you have a job before your arrest?" she asked, shifting tactics. "I just lived life," I answered, offering nothing more, hoping to deflect the attention back to her.

Realizing I wasn't going to crack, Africa launched into her own life story—her case, her family struggles, and the endless problems with her "baby daddy." I was caught between her animated storytelling and my racing thoughts, my mind zooming ahead like a high-performance car on a deserted highway, while my body remained tethered to this cell.

Africa's voice was relentless, and she shared how her bail was only $1,000, a sum that felt so far out of reach for me. I thought to myself, I wish I even had a bail. Then she delved into her tumultuous relationship with her mother, the frustration spilling over as she described her father's sporadic visits. "That n***er," she emphasized with contempt, "acts like driving up from Jersey to the Bronx is a damn marathon. But he's in the club every weekend, living his best life. Nigga, please!"

The N-word rolled off her tongue with such fervor that I felt a twinge of temptation to echo it, to join in the rhythm of her anger. Yet, I remained silent, absorbing the whirlwind of emotions surrounding me. That seemed to be the end of her tirade, but the quiet didn't last long. Three hours later, Mr. Malik approached me, a knowing smirk on his face. "You know Africa's been asking around about you, right? She even thinks you like her."

I blinked in surprise but said nothing. My relationship with Africa was purely circumstantial; I had no issue with anyone's opinions or lifestyles. Instead, I found myself reflecting on my situation, the mistakes I had made that led me to this point.

As I sat there, I looked around at the others—each woman trapped in her own story, the air thick with tales of crack, cocaine, petty theft, and violent crimes. I was different. I was still trying to understand how I ended up in Rikers, searching for a reason that felt just as elusive as the truth behind my own choices. The contrast of our lives was stark, but it also made me ponder the threads that connected us all—fear, desperation, and the longing for redemption.

In that moment of introspection, I realized that while everyone around me had their own battles, I was wrestling with the ghosts of my past. The stories of those in this cramped space served as a mirror, reflecting the complexities of life that had led us all to this place, and the lingering question remained: How do we break free from the cycles that ensnare us?

Zen and the Art of Surviving Rikers

Zen and I had grown close, bonding over our shared status as first-time offenders. Neither of us had a history of run-ins with the law, which provided a strange sense of camaraderie. I joked with her once, "I don't exactly wake up every day thinking, Today's the day I'll yell 'Hands up!' at the cops." Her laughter was infectious, tears streaming down her cheeks as she found humor in our grim reality. It was one of those rare moments where laughter cut through the heavy atmosphere, offering a glimpse of normalcy amidst chaos.

Just then, Africa stormed into our little bubble, followed closely by Mr. Malik. I had just asked Zen when we were heading to the recreation yard, but Africa, never one to be left out, quickly interjected, her voice booming as she launched into a commentary about other inmates.

Then, out of nowhere, she exclaimed, "Did y'all see that n***a's ballsack? That dude's dick was dragging on the floor!" Instantly, all four of us turned, curiosity piqued, as if the spectacle was something we hadn't seen before.

But for me, it wasn't funny. I had experienced violation in the worst way possible, and the thought of body parts dragging on the floor felt like a grotesque reminder of that trauma. The atmosphere shifted, a thick tension settling over the room. We all sensed the potential for violence simmering just beneath the surface, the air heavy with unspoken threats and pent-up frustration.

The typical New York slang filled the air again— threats and trash talk flying back and forth. "Yo, dis na wildin'," one inmate muttered, while another shot back, "Deadass, I'm 'bout to punch this na." Everyone seemed ready to throw down, the anticipation of conflict crackling like static electricity.

But then Mr. Malik's voice cut through the chaos, smooth and commanding. "Yo, chill out! We're not about to start some bullshit over a peep show." His words hung in the air, a reminder that even in the darkest moments, there was power in restraint.

It was as if Malik's calmness acted like a reset button, drawing us back from the brink of escalation. In that moment, I was struck by the absurdity of our situation— how easily laughter could flip into hostility, how quickly camaraderie could turn to chaos.

"Look," he continued, "we're all stuck in here together. Let's not make it worse."

Zen nodded in agreement, her expression softening. "Yeah, we've got enough going on without adding fights to the mix." Her voice held a soothing quality, and I felt grateful for her presence.

Africa rolled her eyes, clearly not in the mood for diplomacy, but even she could sense the shift in energy. Slowly, the group began to disperse, laughter fading into lighter banter as we returned to the mundane reality of our confinement.

I watched as the tension dissolved, wondering how many moments like this were necessary for survival in

Rikers. Moments where humor and humanity could stave off the inevitable darkness. As the day wore on, I realized that navigating this environment required more than just physical endurance; it demanded emotional resilience and a willingness to connect with others, even in the unlikeliest of circumstances.

In this place of uncertainty, I found myself leaning into these relationships—like a delicate balance of survival, laughter, and the unpredictable currents of human emotion. It was in these fleeting connections that I discovered a semblance of peace, a sense of zen that I had never expected to find in a place like Rikers.

Mr. Malik's Tale of Injustice

Mr. Malik leaned back, his expression a mix of frustration and resignation as he began recounting his experiences with the Department of Corrections. "You know," he started, "I was railroaded by the district attorney. My crime didn't warrant a 20-year sentence, but no one believed me." His voice dropped slightly, as if he were letting us in on a secret, an unspoken truth he felt compelled to share. "Now I'm stuck on lifetime probation, and I'm starting to realize how impossible that setup is. It's almost guaranteed you'll violate it at some point."

Curiosity piqued, I asked him what had led to his latest violation. He took a deep breath, clearly recalling the moment that had spiraled into another setback. "I was released on parole with an ankle monitor, right? One day in July, the battery started flashing low, so I plugged it in overnight. I thought everything would be fine when I woke up."

He paused, his brow furrowing as the memory replayed in his mind. "But when I checked it in the morning, it hadn't charged at all. I called my parole officer, but all I got was voicemail. No response. I was panicking, knowing that I had to take action."

Malik's voice grew more animated as he recounted his desperate attempt to rectify the situation. "By 4:00 p.m., I decided I had to jump on the train and head to the parole office. I thought, maybe if I can just explain it to someone before the weekend, I'd be okay."

"But when I got there around 5:00 p.m., the place was packed," he continued, shaking his head in disbelief. "They were all celebrating a retirement party. My parole officer was right in the middle of it, laughing, eating, just enjoying himself. I tapped him on the shoulder and explained what had happened with the monitor, but he barely looked up. Just told me to go home and that he'd deal with it on Monday."

Malik's frustration bubbled over as he finished his story. "That's how it is, man. They don't care. It's a setup." He glanced around at the others, his eyes filled with a mix of anger and disbelief. It was clear that he felt trapped in a system that seemed designed to fail him.

As he spoke, I could see the weariness etched into his features, the weight of years spent navigating a labyrinthine justice system. In that moment, it became painfully apparent how easily a single misstep could lead to dire consequences, how the very mechanisms meant to support rehabilitation often became instruments of oppression.

His story clicked with me, reflecting a reality that many of us in this place were grappling with. The sense of injustice and helplessness echoed through our conversations, reminding us all that in Rikers, we were more than just our charges; we were caught in a web of circumstances that could ensnare anyone. Malik's tale was a reminder of how fragile our lives could be when faced with a system that prioritized punishment over understanding.

Mr. Malik's Unending Struggle

Malik's voice was heavy with frustration as he shared the next chapter of his ordeal. After reporting the dead battery on his ankle monitor, Monday came and went without any response from his parole officer. He tried to keep his life on track, assuming things were resolved, but trouble came knocking soon enough.

"A couple of weeks later, I was traveling with my ex," he said, rubbing his hands together as if trying to shake off the memory. "We got into an argument, and she called the cops on me." His expression darkened. "That's all it takes—a cop showing up, even if you didn't do anything. That's a parole violation, just like that."

The call to the police set off a chain reaction, with Malik accused not only of police contact but also of tampering with his ankle monitor. "I didn't touch the damn thing," he said, his voice tinged with both anger and exhaustion. "But once they think you did, that's it. You're guilty until proven innocent."

The next day, Malik reported to the parole office, expecting the usual 15-day stint in jail for a minor violation. But this time was different. "They told me I'd get 15 days, but the case dragged on for *months*," he said, clenching his jaw. "Four months, just sitting there waiting. They didn't care how long it took."

He leaned forward, his eyes filled with bitterness. "They use us like pawns. They know if they keep you locked up long enough, you'll get desperate. You'll plead to anything, just to get out."

Malik admitted that this experience had pushed him to the edge. "I've been thinking about running," he confessed quietly, as if the thought alone carried a heavy weight. "Not something I'd recommend for anyone—

especially someone my age, pushing 50. But, honestly, what's left for me?"

His voice trailed off as he reflected on his circumstances. "When you come from where I come from, you learn quick. They say, 'Follow the rules,' but when the rules are set up to make you fail, what can you really do?" He shook his head. "It's easy for people on the outside to say, 'Just stay clean.' They don't know what it's like to be set up to lose from the start."

Malik looked down at his hands, almost as if he were holding the weight of his life in his palms. "I've never been anywhere—not outside the U.S., not even to see another part of the world. This country is all I've known." He exhaled deeply, resignation settling into his voice. "But I already know how my story ends."

In that moment, it became clear that Malik wasn't just recounting the past—he was wrestling with the bleak reality of a future that seemed predetermined. His story wasn't just about parole violations or the justice system. It was about a life trapped within invisible bars long before he ever set foot in jail.

Interrupted Conversations

I tried to process Malik's situation, but as always in Rikers, my thoughts were cut short—again. Miss Africa had a knack for barging into conversations. Earlier, she interrupted me mid-sentence while I was talking with Jennifer. It's almost impossible to hold a thought without someone butting in here, like peace is something you have to fight for.

Jennifer, though, was patient. She never forced her words into a conversation but waited until the moment was right. That quiet patience was rare in a place like this. Even though she didn't say much, her silence spoke volumes, and I found myself opening up to her little by little.

One day, I shared a piece of my story with her. "I came to the U.S. when I was 12," I began slowly. "And just a year and three months later, I became an orphan."

Jennifer leaned in slightly, her calm gaze letting me know I had her full attention. I hadn't told many people about my past, but something about Jennifer made it easier to talk.

"My dad worked day and night to provide for us," I continued. "My mom stayed home to take care of us kids. Life was simple. But everything changed on my father's 45th birthday."

I felt myself drifting into the memory as I spoke. "That morning, Joel—my dad's best friend—called. It was 4:00 a.m., and it was pouring rain outside. Joel said he needed help with his car, some kind of breakdown on his way to work. My dad hadn't planned to leave the house. He wanted to celebrate, relax for once. But Joel kept calling."

I could see it clearly in my mind: the old landline ringing shrilly in the dark. My mother, startled from sleep, rolled over and answered it. My parents always kept the phone loud in case there was an emergency call from family back home. Even in their deepest sleep, they could wake to that sound.

"Joel was persistent, but my mom wasn't having it," I told Jennifer. "'Not tonight,' she told my dad. She didn't like the idea of him driving in that weather, especially not on his birthday."

I paused, the weight of the memory settling over me. "They argued a little—not in anger, just the kind of back-and-forth married couples do. I remember my dad laughing quietly, like it was all a joke. Even Princess—my baby sister—stirred in her crib. She was only three months old then. They named her after the queen of England."

For a moment, the memory filled the silence between Jennifer and me, as vivid as if I were back there. The sound of rain tapping against the windows, my parents' voices weaving between playfulness and concern.

"I think about that moment a lot," I said, almost to myself. "How things might have been different if Joel hadn't called... or if my dad had just stayed in bed."

Jennifer gave me a slow, understanding nod. She didn't rush to offer advice or pity, which I appreciated. The silence that followed wasn't the heavy, suffocating kind I'd grown used to at Rikers—it felt lighter, like a shared moment of acknowledgment.

But the moment didn't last. In a place like this, quiet never does.

Reflection

I trailed off, lost in the memory, the edges of it blurring into the present. Jennifer didn't fill the space with words—just a quiet nod, like she understood without needing to say anything. There's something about the way life unfolds, how tiny moments and decisions, barely noticeable at the time, end up shaping the entire course of things.

I thought about how often conversations get derailed in here—how stories remain unfinished, scattered like broken glass. Africa's constant chatter and Malik's battles with the system always barged in, forcing attention away. But the truth is, we're all trying to piece together our stories from fragments, sorting through memories and mistakes, searching for meaning amid the chaos.

The interruptions are endless, like background noise that never stops. And yet, I realized something: the rare moments of silence feel different here. They're not just gaps between words—they're spaces where everything hangs heavy, where thoughts are raw and real.

In a place like this, silence is both a curse and a gift. It can swallow you whole, suffocating in its stillness. But it can also be a refuge, a moment of peace in a storm that never seems to end.

The Day Everything Changed

On the morning of November 5, 1994, the house felt oddly still, as if it were holding its breath. The phone had been on hold for at least 15 minutes, and my father—always the one to make decisions—finally broke the silence. "Honey, you're welcome to join me if you like, but I'm leaving now," he said calmly.

My mother knew him too well to argue. When my father made up his mind, there was no changing it. But she wasn't about to let him venture into the storm alone at 4:00 a.m. She moved with purpose, faster than I'd ever seen, determined to accompany him. (That moment became a family joke—Mom, rushing out in her nightclothes but somehow managing to keep her dignity intact.)

Before leaving, she turned to me with a simple instruction: "You're in charge while we're gone. Keep the house quiet." I was almost 15 then, the second oldest of our 10 siblings. Mom trusted me to maintain order, though we all knew my older brother—16, almost 17—was the real authority in the house. Everyone looked to him, and in truth, so did I.

Our youngest, Princess, was still sound asleep when our parents slipped out the door. We didn't think much of their absence at first. It was my father's 45th birthday, and we assumed they might stop somewhere after helping Joel—maybe picking up a cake or some takeout for later. It was the kind of simple plan you don't question.

But as the hours dragged on, an uneasy feeling began to settle in. At first, we busied ourselves—tidying up, entertaining the little ones, trying not to think about the clock ticking. Yet with each passing hour, that feeling grew heavier, like the weight of a storm cloud hovering just overhead.

Evening approached, and still, there was no sign of them.

Waiting for the News

By evening, they still hadn't come back. It was strange, unsettling. They never stayed out this long without checking in. My brother wore that familiar worried look— the kind that made everyone uneasy because it meant things might not be okay. I tried to keep the younger kids distracted, but their restless energy gnawed at my nerves. Honestly, I was just as restless as they were, pacing in and out of rooms, listening for any sound that might signal their return.

We clung to hopeful explanations. Maybe they made an extra stop. Maybe they lost track of time. But as night crept in and the hours stretched, those comforting excuses started to unravel. Anxiety settled over us, thick and stifling. My brother's unease began to infect the rest of us, spreading like wildfire through our small, crowded house.

Around 8:00 p.m., we made the call we hoped we wouldn't have to—our Aunt Janet. Aunt Janet wasn't just family; she was a second mother, the kind of person who knew when something was wrong before you even said it out loud. As soon as we told her what was going on, her voice sharpened with concern. "Your mother would *never* leave you all without calling," she said, her words firm and laced with dread. "Something's not right."

That was all Aunt Janet needed to spring into action. She went into crisis mode, spending the next few hours on the phone, calling anyone who might have answers—neighbors, friends, even the police station. Every few hours, she would call us back, her voice steady but tense. "No news yet," she'd say. "But don't worry. We'll find them."

We stayed up all night, waiting for any word. No one slept—not even Princess, who sensed that something was off despite being just a baby. The house, usually filled with the lively noise of ten siblings, felt hollow. Every small sound—the creak of a floorboard, the hum of the refrigerator—felt like it might bring news. But the hours dragged on in unbearable silence, and all we could do was wait, trapped in the uncertainty.

The Knock on the Door

The following morning, just after our last call with Aunt Janet, a knock echoed through the house. My little sister, thinking it was finally our parents, bolted to the door. "They're here!" she squealed, her voice bright with relief.

But when she swung the door open, her excitement dissolved instantly. Standing on the doorstep was a police officer, his face grim. The hope that had briefly filled the air vanished as quickly as it had come, replaced by an icy knot in my stomach.

"Who's in charge here?" the officer asked, scanning the room.

Without missing a beat, my brother stepped forward, standing tall despite the fear flickering in his eyes. He was trying to project strength for all of us, though we knew he was just as scared.

The officer gave a slight nod and gestured for my brother to step outside. I instinctively followed, but before I could make it out the door, my brother turned, his jaw tight. "Go back inside," he said in a low, commanding voice. There was no arguing with him when he spoke like that. Reluctantly, I obeyed, retreating into the house, my heart thudding against my ribs.

From the window, we watched, breathless, as the officer spoke with him. Their conversation was too far away to hear, but the weight of it hung in the air like a storm cloud. The officer's expression was unreadable, but my brother stood still, his face solemn and unflinching. Every so often, the officer pulled out a notepad and jotted something down, adding to the sense that something terrible had happened.

The minutes dragged, stretching unbearably long. Inside, we huddled together—silent, anxious. My younger siblings clung to one another, stealing nervous glances through the window, hoping against hope that it wasn't as bad as it seemed.

But deep down, we knew. The slump in my brother's shoulders gave it away, the slight sag as the officer spoke words too heavy for him to bear alone. Even before he turned back toward the house, we understood: Whatever news had arrived on that doorstep, it was going to change everything.

The Moment Everything Changed

When my brother finally stepped inside, his face was pale, and his eyes glistened with tears he hadn't yet shed. He didn't need to say anything—we knew.

Our parents were gone.

In that instant, everything familiar, everything that made life feel safe, crumbled. The house—once filled with warmth and laughter—felt hollow and cold, as if their presence had vanished along with the news. It was like the walls themselves had lost their strength, and all that remained was emptiness. Life as we knew it was over.

The Day We Lost Everything

From the window, we had seen the officer move closer to my brother. What we didn't expect was the way he reached out and wrapped my brother in a hug. They stood there for a long moment, two strangers bound by the unbearable weight of loss. When the officer finally stepped away, my brother was left alone on the porch, standing in stunned silence.

We couldn't wait for him to come inside. The door was already wide open, and we rushed to meet him. But as soon as my brother crossed the threshold, everything collapsed.

He tried to wrap me in a hug, but instead, his legs buckled. He fell to the floor, crumpling under the weight of what he had been holding in. His body shook as he sobbed, gasping for breath between deep, aching cries. He clutched at his chest, as if trying to physically hold himself together—but he couldn't.

He looked up at me, his face wet with tears, and whispered the words that would haunt me forever:

"They're dead."

Everything inside me broke at once. I let out a wail, the kind of cry that comes from a place deeper than sorrow—a cry from the soul. My brother, only 17 years old, was crumbling right in front of me, barely able to keep himself from shattering completely.

Our 12-year-old brother stood nearby, frozen and trembling, as if the very ground beneath him had given way.

The weight of the moment was too much for his small frame to bear, and he seemed as lost as the rest of us.

The phone still dangled off the hook—we hadn't thought to hang it up in the chaos. Aunt Janet had been listening the entire time, quietly bearing witness to the unraveling of our world. Her voice came through the receiver, faint and trembling.

"I'm on my way," she whispered.

We stayed there on the floor, tangled in grief, waiting for her, but knowing even her presence couldn't fix what had just been broken. Nothing ever would.

"They Are Ghosts Now"

My 4-year-old sister, her innocence still untouched by the harsh realities of life, looked up at us with wide, confused eyes. "Is brother in trouble with the police man?" she asked, her voice soft and uncertain, as if the world had suddenly turned strange and unfamiliar.

Our 6-year-old sister, usually so full of laughter, looked at her solemnly and replied in a way that shattered my heart. "No. Mom and Dad are ghosts now."

Her words hung in the air like a heavy fog, suffocating the tiny bit of hope we had left. I wanted to scoop them both into my arms, to hold them tightly and protect them from the pain that was crashing over us like relentless waves. But I felt paralyzed by grief, overwhelmed by the reality that had just set in.

From this moment on, everything had changed. I wasn't just a sister anymore; I was now a mother to eight siblings. The weight of responsibility settled heavily on my shoulders, a burden I never asked for. And my brother—he had suddenly transformed from my sibling into their father, thrust into a role he was not ready to assume.

As I stood there, my heart breaking for my sisters' innocence and for the burden that lay ahead of us, I knew we would have to navigate this new reality together. But the thought of it felt impossibly heavy, as if the very air around us had thickened with the gravity of our loss. We were now a family of ghosts ourselves—haunted by memories, marked by absence, and forever changed by the tragedy that had shattered our lives.

Forced to Grow Up Overnight

Coming from a different culture, we were raised with strong values that emphasized the importance of family privacy: you don't share your family's struggles with outsiders. Our belief was that family problems stayed within the family, hidden from the outside world. But now, we were suddenly thrust into a harsh reality that expected us to navigate life without the safety net of our parents.

Aunt Janet, despite her unwavering love for us and her determination to help, simply couldn't afford to take us all in financially. With no other options on the horizon, my brother had no choice but to step up and take responsibility. The weight of that responsibility was staggering, especially for a 17-year-old who was still grappling with the loss of our parents.

Losing our parents was already more than we could bear; the thought of being split up in foster care was a fate worse than death. No matter how hard things got, my brother was resolute in his determination to keep us together. He would face the challenges head-on, shielding us from the harsh realities outside our small world, even as he struggled to cope with his own grief.

We quickly learned that life wouldn't wait for us to catch our breath. With every passing day, the weight of our situation grew heavier, and we were forced to adapt, to become more than just children mourning the loss of our parents. We had to become a family unit, relying on one another for support and strength. Each of us had a role to play, whether it was keeping the younger ones entertained or helping my brother manage the household. We became each other's lifelines in a world that suddenly felt so big and so unforgiving.

In those early days, I often caught myself staring at my siblings, trying to memorize their faces, their laughter, their little quirks. I knew that we had to hold onto those moments, to cling to our shared memories, because they were all we had left of our parents. We were navigating uncharted waters, learning to grow up overnight in a world that didn't seem to care about our loss. But amidst the pain and chaos, we found solace in each other. Together, we would face whatever came next.

A Brother's Sacrifice

At just 17 years old, my brother made the monumental decision to drop out of school and take on the responsibility of providing for our family. He got a job at a local shampoo factory, working the graveyard shift. Each day, he left the house at 4:00 a.m., taking three trains just to reach work on time. His shifts lasted 12 hours, six days a week, and for all that labor, he earned a mere $750 every two weeks. I knew this not just from his words, but from my own role as the second oldest, managing our meager food budget.

There wasn't much to manage, really. Our family was living on the edge, with no extra money for luxuries and no stocked pantry to rely on. Every dollar was precious, and I learned quickly how to stretch our limited resources. Our rent for the cramped studio apartment we had to move into was $525 a month, which left us little else for necessities. Every meal was planned down to the last crumb, and I quickly became adept at creating filling dishes from whatever ingredients we could scrounge together.

The absence of our parents left us isolated; there were no neighbors to lean on for support and no friends to confide in. The only friends we had were each other, united in our shared loss and struggle. With ten siblings in the house, there was hardly any room for anyone else, emotionally or physically.

Despite the burden of responsibility, my brother rarely complained. He wore his sacrifices like armor, protecting us from the weight of our circumstances. I admired him for his resilience; he somehow managed to keep a smile on his face even when exhaustion lined his features. I often found myself wishing I could help him bear the weight he carried, but my role was to support him and the younger siblings, ensuring we held together as a family.

As I cooked and organized our meager meals, I couldn't help but reflect on the enormity of my brother's sacrifice. He had given up his childhood to step into a role he had never asked for, and yet, he did it willingly. I knew that each shift he worked, each sacrifice he made, was a testament to his love for us. He was a brother, a father figure, and a hero all rolled into one, navigating the challenges of adulthood at an age when he should have been enjoying the freedom of youth. In those moments, I vowed to honor his sacrifices by making the best of our situation, no matter how hard it became.

Survival Without Support

The school system offered no recognition of our profound loss. There were no grief counseling sessions, no therapy options, and no one to confide in about our struggles. We were expected to carry on with our lives as if nothing had happened, a pressure that felt unbearable. Yet amidst this silence, there was a glimmer of hope in the form of Mr. Jerry, one of my father's friends. He stepped in during our darkest hours, ensuring we had a way to get to school each day. He made it his mission to keep us engaged with our education, even when everything else in our lives felt like it was crumbling around us.

The Salvation Army became our lifeline, providing us with used clothes and shoes to keep us warm during the cold months. Their generosity was a blessing, yet it was hard to shake the feeling of isolation that lingered. We wore donated clothes with gratitude, but there was an unspoken weight that accompanied them—a reminder of our circumstances, a stark contrast to the lives of our peers.

Despite the kindness we received, there was a persistent sense that we were on our own. The community around us was unaware of the turmoil we faced behind closed doors. At school, we learned to wear masks, smiling when we needed to and laughing at jokes to blend in, while inside we were grappling with grief and survival. The weight of responsibility hung over us, and I felt an urgency to protect my siblings from the harsh realities we faced.

Every day was a struggle to maintain normalcy, but Mr. Jerry's support reminded us that we weren't completely alone. He would check in on us, encouraging us to stay focused on our studies, and sometimes he would surprise us with small gestures—a new backpack, a lunchbox, or even a few treats. Those moments of kindness felt like rays of light cutting through the darkness, fueling our determination to push forward.

We learned to navigate our new reality together, growing closer in the process. As we relied on each other for emotional support, I realized that while we may have felt abandoned by the world, we had each other. That bond became our strongest source of resilience, reminding us that even in the depths of despair, love and family could be a powerful force for survival.

A Silent Struggle

Life in that tiny apartment was a constant battle, yet we rarely voiced our struggles. Complaining was a luxury we couldn't afford; every moment was consumed by the urgency of survival. My siblings and I quickly learned to keep our pain and grief locked away, hidden beneath the surface. We didn't talk about our parents or the profound loss that lingered like a shadow over our lives. The weight of it was too heavy, and the world around us seemed to demand that we simply carry on as if nothing had changed.

My brother worked tirelessly, pushing himself to the brink of exhaustion as he toiled away at the factory. He bore the weight of our family's financial responsibilities, sacrificing his youth for our survival. Meanwhile, I did my best to hold the household together, balancing the needs of my younger siblings with my own schooling. There were days when I felt overwhelmed, but I had no choice; my siblings relied on me, and I couldn't let them down.

Our home was filled with the laughter and chaos of children, but beneath the surface, we were navigating a storm of emotions that we never shared with anyone outside our walls. We didn't bring friends home—not because we didn't want companionship, but because there simply wasn't room for anyone else in our cramped space. Our lives had become a delicate dance of responsibilities; while the younger kids were at school, I juggled my own classes with the care of our little ones, trying to ensure they felt loved and supported.

Every day was a test of resilience. We didn't have the luxury of expressing our grief or seeking help from others. Instead, we focused on making ends meet, finding ways to lighten each other's burdens even as we carried our own. The small moments of joy we shared—a shared meal, a game, or a simple laugh—became precious treasures, keeping the darkness at bay for just a little longer.

In that silence, we forged an unbreakable bond. We were each other's confidants, holding space for one another in a world that felt isolating and harsh. Even in our struggles, we found strength in our togetherness, learning that while the pain of our past was ever-present, the love we shared was a powerful force that could help us endure whatever lay ahead.

Holding On to Each Other

Every day was a relentless fight for survival, but my brother and I were resolute in our mission to keep our family together. We had already lost so much—our parents, our sense of security, and the innocence of childhood. The thought of losing each other too was simply unimaginable. In moments when the weight of our circumstances felt unbearably heavy, we leaned on one another, drawing strength from the unbreakable bond we shared.

We carved out small rituals to anchor ourselves amidst the chaos. At dinner, we gathered around the table, sharing what little food we had and filling the air with laughter, however forced it sometimes felt. Those moments became our lifeline, reminders that even in the midst of grief, joy could still flicker to life. We took turns telling stories—about our parents, our childhood, or dreams for the future—keeping their memory alive while also envisioning a brighter tomorrow.

Despite the darkness that often threatened to engulf us, we never stopped believing that things could get better. Each morning, we woke up to the same harsh realities, but we faced them together, united in our determination to rise above our circumstances. The world outside may have seen us as just another family struggling to get by, but within our walls, we nurtured a spirit of resilience.

Through it all, we remained a family—flawed, broken, and grieving, yet steadfastly together. In our shared silence, we found solace; in our collective struggle, we discovered hope. Our love for one another became our sanctuary, a safe harbor against the storms that raged around us. As we navigated the complexities of life without our parents, we learned to redefine what family meant, embracing the imperfections that came with it.

Together, we held on, refusing to let go, believing that as long as we had each other, there was a flicker of light in the darkness, a possibility for healing, and a path forward. No matter how bleak our situation felt, we clung to the truth that love could endure even the most devastating losses, weaving a thread of hope through the fabric of our lives.

Life After Loss

After our parents' tragic passing, my brother stepped up as our new father figure, providing me with $100 a month to feed our family of ten, which included myself. It felt surreal, as if nothing had truly changed in our lives— like our parents were simply on an extended vacation. We navigated each day with the same routines, tried to maintain a sense of normalcy, and often fell into the rhythm of survival, even as the weight of grief lingered heavily in the air.

I returned to school, but I had to craft a different reality to shield myself from the truth. I confided in my favorite school counselor, telling her that my mother was sick and that I was her caretaker. It felt necessary to shield my siblings from any extra scrutiny, especially since they were already grappling with their own grief. I fabricated a story about having a child with no father, explaining why I couldn't attend school during the day. It was a fragile lie, but one I hoped would help me keep my head above water.

Thanks to my late father's friend, Mr. Jeremy, who had always been a pillar of support, I managed to enroll in night classes. Suddenly, my days were filled with the chaos of motherhood while my nights transformed into a quest for education. I juggled diaper changes, cooking meals, and comforting my siblings during the day, and then, as the sun dipped below the horizon, I shifted gears, diving into textbooks and assignments under the soft glow of a lamp.

There were moments when exhaustion threatened to overwhelm me, when the weight of responsibilities felt unbearable. I often stole glances at my siblings, each one carrying their own burden of loss, and I pushed through, reminding myself that we were all in this together. My brother worked tirelessly, and I did my best to hold everything together, ensuring that the little ones felt some semblance of normalcy, even as we lived in a world defined by absence.

Each night class felt like a small victory, a reminder that despite our circumstances, I could still pursue my dreams. Yet, as I walked home under the starry sky, the silence would seep back in, a stark reminder of what we had lost. But in that silence, I also found strength—the knowledge that I was doing this for them, for us. I clung to the hope that one day, things would get better, that the love we shared would help us heal, and that we would find our way back to a life filled with light, laughter, and the possibility of a future.

Facing Challenges

One day, as I walked my sisters to school, I overheard a teacher from the first period mention they needed to speak to my parent. I muffled a sarcastic comment under my breath, thinking, *Good luck with that.* The weight of their expectations hung in the air, reminding me of all that we had lost. As I returned home, the floodgates opened, and I drowned in tears, overwhelmed by the responsibilities pressing down on my shoulders.

For 21 years, my brother had taken on the role of our father, a role that no one should have to fill at such a young age. His sacrifices shaped our lives in profound ways, allowing my younger sister to pursue her medical degree and paving the way for all ten of us to achieve our dreams. It wasn't easy—there were countless nights when we fell asleep hungry or days when we fought to stay afloat in a system that often overlooked us. Yet, against all odds, we persevered.

In time, we each carved out our own paths. I became a medical doctor, driven by a desire to heal others and honor the sacrifices my brother made. Another sibling embraced the nursing profession, ensuring compassionate care for those in need. One turned their passion for home decor into a successful bed-and-bath store, while another found their niche in real estate, helping families find their forever homes. We had one sibling who thrived in home development, transforming spaces and lives, and another dedicated to shaping young minds as a school teacher.

In our own unique ways, we all made it, defying the odds stacked against us. The journey was far from perfect, marked by struggles and sacrifices, but we held tight to the belief that family could overcome anything. We found strength in each other, drawing on the love that had bound us even through the darkest times. Every graduation, every achievement felt like a tribute to our parents—a testament that their legacy lived on through us.

As I reflect on our journey, I realize that while we faced challenges that would have broken many, we emerged stronger, united, and capable of achieving our dreams. The bond we share is unshakeable, a reminder that even in the face of adversity, hope and resilience can light the way forward.

Surviving and Thriving

Despite our struggles, we understood that none of us was perfect. We didn't make excuses for our behavior; instead, we learned from it. Reflecting on our past, we realized the importance of acknowledging our experiences rather than hiding from them. Each scar, each tear shed, had shaped us into who we were—a resilient family navigating life's unpredictable waters together.

In this new chapter of my life, I found myself at Rikers Island, a place far removed from the dreams I once held. The irony of my situation wasn't lost on me. I started attending meetings, speaking openly about my experiences, and sharing my story with those around me. I hoped that by sharing, I could help others find their voice amid their struggles.

In the dining room before our meeting one day, I observed the women around me—many were hardened by their circumstances, while others, like a girl who had earned the nickname "Africa," were there to fight against the odds that had brought them to this point. Each one carried their own story, a tapestry of survival woven with pain and resilience.

As I sat with Zen, the atmosphere around us was charged with a blend of anticipation and anxiety. Jain approached me, signaling that I would appear at the prayer table. I didn't move; instead, I closed my eyes and began to pray, seeking solace and strength in the chaos surrounding us.

Upon opening my eyes, I was jolted back into the moment by someone yelling, "What the FUCK!" from the prayer table. The voice belonged to a girl nicknamed ET, who hailed from South Africa. Her outburst was a shocking reminder that we were all still navigating a world filled with chaos and conflict, even within these walls meant for rehabilitation.

In that moment, I recognized the common thread binding us all together—each of us was searching for understanding, healing, and a way to thrive amidst the struggles we faced. I realized that our stories, as painful as they were, could be our greatest source of strength. We were not just survivors; we were thrivers, each carving out our own path toward redemption and hope, determined to break free from the chains that bound us, both physically and emotionally.

Unexpected Calls

It was early morning on September 4, around 5:00 a.m., when I heard the officer in the bubble calling names for a headcount. When she called my name, my heart raced, a mix of confusion and anxiety swelling within me. What could this mean so early in the day? My mind raced through the possibilities, each scenario more unsettling than the last.

Court Day Realities

I was feeling uneasy because the last time I had been in court, the judge set my next appearance for September 8, 2024, at 9:30 a.m. So when I heard the bubble officer announce my name at 5:00 a.m. on September 4, I was confused. It felt like a Catholic priest calling someone to service, and I jumped out of my seat, running to the window, asking the officer, "Did you call my name for court?"

She shot me a look that seemed filled with malice, a chilling reminder of the power dynamics at play in this environment. Her eyes told me everything I needed to know—she wasn't interested in explaining anything. I realized she was too tired to think or speak; all she could do was yell and stare, the weight of her authority pressing down like an iron shackle.

Tired of being bullied by her attitude, I stood my ground. I wasn't going to let fear dictate my reactions. "I just want to know if I'm going to court today," I insisted, trying to keep my voice steady. My heart pounded, each beat echoing in the cramped space of my mind. I could feel the tension building in the air around me as the other inmates watched, their faces a mixture of curiosity and sympathy.

For a moment, I wondered if standing up for myself would make things worse or better. In this world where vulnerability often led to more pain, I chose to be defiant, to reclaim a small piece of my agency. "I deserve to know why I'm being called," I said, my voice firm despite the unease curling in my stomach.

Her glare deepened, and she finally snapped back, "You'll find out when you get there." With that, she turned her back, moving on to the next name on the list, leaving me to grapple with the unknown. In that instant, I understood: this was a world ruled by unpredictability, where power was wielded with indifference. The uncertainty of the coming hours felt suffocating, but I clung to the hope that somehow, I would navigate this day, no matter what lay ahead.

Emotional Turmoil

As I prepared for court, I felt a tumultuous mix of emotions swirling within me—anxiety, hope, dread, and a desperate longing to go home. I knew the judge held the power to release me, but the thought of the ordeal ahead filled me with trepidation. The process felt like a cruel ritual, one that stripped away any semblance of dignity I might have clung to.

Enduring humiliating procedures was part of the routine. I had to stay alert in front of the officers, squatting down and coughing three times to prove I wasn't hiding anything. Each cough felt like a betrayal of my own body, a reminder that I was now under constant scrutiny, a mere number in a system designed to break rather than to heal.

Once I was finally out, I would be handcuffed with two other inmates, crammed into a cage on a bus for what felt like an eternity. The cramped space felt suffocating as we jostled against one another, the metal bars of our confinement a stark reminder of our reality. The bus ride would last 30 to 45 minutes, filled with an unsettling silence that seemed to amplify the unspoken fears among us. We left the jail at 6:00 a.m., and the cold morning air felt like a harsh slap against my skin, a reminder that I was stepping into a world that had grown increasingly alien.

Arriving at court by 6:45 a.m. was just the beginning. Once inside, we'd be ushered to a holding cell behind the courtroom, where the stench of sweat and despair hung heavy in the air. We'd sit there, waiting and watching the minutes crawl by until 11:00 a.m., the hour when we'd finally see the judge. The time stretched infinitely, a test of endurance and patience, with each tick of the clock echoing in my mind.

After the brief court appearance, I'd be given a meager lunch break from 12:00 p.m. to 1:00 p.m. The food was uninspired and bland, a stark contrast to the emotional turmoil I felt inside. As I ate, the reality of the situation settled in deeper—this wasn't just a bad dream; it was my life now.

The rest of the inmates would start being called back to the holding cell, a reminder that we were all in this together, yet utterly alone in our struggles. By the time we were all called back, it was often around 7:00 p.m. The day stretched on, an agonizing reminder of how time could feel both fleeting and endless in this place. Each moment spent waiting, each procedure endured, reinforced the knowledge that I was fighting not just for my freedom, but for the sense of self that had been so cruelly stripped away.

Harsh Conditions

Throughout this ordeal, the conditions we faced were grueling and dehumanizing. We received no food or drink, a cruel punishment that only heightened our sense of desperation. The toilet in our cell barely functioned, a grim reminder of our circumstances, forcing us to ask the officer for hand sanitizer every five minutes. With no way to wash our hands after using the filthy, unflushed toilet, we were left feeling dirty and vulnerable, trapped in a cycle of discomfort and humiliation.

When we finally returned to our dorm, it would often be around 10:00 p.m., but the journey back could stretch even longer. For those of us whose cases were in Brooklyn or the Bronx, the return might not happen until 1:00 a.m. or 2:00 a.m., adding insult to injury after a long day in court. By the time we saw the judge, exhaustion would weigh heavily on our bodies and minds. The dreariness of our environment seeped into our souls, making it difficult to muster even a shred of hope.

Many inmates, desperate to return to the relative safety of the dorm, would plead guilty just to escape the grueling process, choosing the false comfort of confinement over the uncertainty of what lay ahead. The system had a way of breaking down our resolve, forcing us to make choices we never thought we would have to consider.

Finding a moment of respite was nearly impossible. A nap on the filthy mattress was a rare luxury, usually lasting only 10 to 15 minutes before someone started a fight, disrupting any chance of rest. We were perpetually on edge, hyper-aware of our surroundings, as the tension in the air became palpable. Each day felt like a battle against both the system and ourselves.

Going to court required not just physical endurance, but mental preparation. It was a journey fraught with challenges—one that stripped away our dignity and reduced us to mere cases, numbers in a system that often felt indifferent to our suffering. Each step through the process was a reminder of the harsh realities we faced, yet we held onto the flickering hope that one day, this nightmare would end, and we could reclaim our lives.

Harsh Conditions

Throughout this ordeal, the conditions we faced were grueling and dehumanizing. We received no food or drink, a cruel punishment that only heightened our sense of desperation. The toilet in our cell barely functioned, a grim reminder of our circumstances, forcing us to ask the officer for hand sanitizer every five minutes. With no way to wash our hands after using the filthy, unflushed toilet, we were left feeling dirty and vulnerable, trapped in a cycle of discomfort and humiliation.

When we finally returned to our dorm, it would often be around 10:00 p.m., but the journey back could stretch even longer. For those of us whose cases were in Brooklyn or the Bronx, the return might not happen until 1:00 a.m. or 2:00 a.m., adding insult to injury after a long day in court. By the time we saw the judge, exhaustion would weigh heavily on our bodies and minds. The dreariness of our environment seeped into our souls, making it difficult to muster even a shred of hope.

Many inmates, desperate to return to the relative safety of the dorm, would plead guilty just to escape the grueling process, choosing the false comfort of confinement over the uncertainty of what lay ahead. The system had a way of breaking down our resolve, forcing us to make choices we never thought we would have to consider.

Finding a moment of respite was nearly impossible. A nap on the filthy mattress was a rare luxury, usually lasting only 10 to 15 minutes before someone started a fight, disrupting any chance of rest. We were perpetually on edge, hyper-aware of our surroundings, as the tension in the air became palpable. Each day felt like a battle against both the system and ourselves.

Going to court required not just physical endurance, but mental preparation. It was a journey fraught with challenges—one that stripped away our dignity and reduced us to mere cases, numbers in a system that often felt indifferent to our suffering. Each step through the process was a reminder of the harsh realities we faced, yet we held onto the flickering hope that one day, this nightmare would end, and we could reclaim our lives.

Anticipation of the Courtroom

While sitting in the holding cell behind the courtroom, the atmosphere felt charged with tension. I could hear the heavy clang of food trays and the unmistakable sound of keys rattling. It was as if they were preparing to break an inmate out of Fort Knox or gearing up to take Osama Bin Laden to trial. Each noise resonated through the cell, amplifying my anxiety as I braced myself for what was to come.

Courtroom Encounter

Then, a very cheerful female officer—whom I assumed was a woman—called my name so loudly that it startled Crackhead Alexis, who jumped off her nap couch and landed hard on the bare concrete floor. Alexis was a mess, her worries about her sentence palpable. She was desperate to enter a drug program instead of facing more jail time, her heavy feet dangling as she grumbled about the officer's volume.

"Did she really have to scream my name that loud?" I thought, bemused. This was New York, after all; everyone was loud. I stood up in the cell, my heart racing as I anxiously awaited the door to open.

When it finally did, the officer handcuffed me and led me into the courtroom. As I walked in, I was greeted by a white man with salt-and-pepper hair, my court-appointed lawyer. He approached me with a warm smile, asking if I had enough time to discuss everything with him. But before I could respond, the judge cut in sharply.

"Be quiet," he commanded. "Only your lawyer can speak on your behalf."

Frustration washed over me as I absorbed the formalities that surrounded me. I was drowning in a sea of procedures that felt designed to strip away any sense of agency I had left. Then, the officer handed me a waiver, a document that authorized the state to expedite my transfer to the court where my warrant originated.

"Ma'am, can you take off the handcuffs so the defendant can sign the waiver?" the officer requested.

The officer replied that she was working court duty and couldn't remove the handcuffs due to staff shortages, a familiar refrain that felt like a cruel joke. My lawyer stepped in, suggesting that sometimes he could sign the waiver on behalf of the defendant. The judge then turned to me, his gaze piercing through the tension, asking if I permitted my lawyer to sign for me since I was still handcuffed.

In that moment, I felt the weight of the system pressing down on me. I nodded, the sense of helplessness enveloping me as I realized just how little control I had over my own life.

Despair in the Courtroom

I felt a profound silence settle over me as I stared at the judge, my throat closing up, words trapped inside. Tears fell freely, reflecting the helplessness I felt as I was yet again silenced. "The defendant agrees for the lawyer to sign the expedition waiver," he said, noting it for the record, and just like that, my so-called attorney signed. The ink barely dry, I was back in the holding cell, waiting in isolation for the next transfer back to jail. The wait was endless, each minute stretching into a hollow eternity.

The walk back to the basement jail cell felt blurred, like my mind had checked out, unable to process the weight of everything pressing down on me. No one recorded that moment; it felt like a void. An overwhelming sense of despair hit me, and I began to wonder if this really was the end. I cried until my tears ran dry, and as my thoughts darkened, I began to imagine what life would be like if I simply ran—or if I ended it altogether.

I looked around and spotted the handle on a window. A flicker of impulse surged through me as I wondered if it could somehow be a way out. But reality quickly doused my thoughts: it wasn't long enough to do the job. I tested the window and found it was fiberglass—hard plastic, unbreakable. As I sat back down, I toyed with fantasies of escape, wondering what dangers might lurk below if I could ever make it out. "This is New York," I thought. "Could be anything down there. Rats, alligators… worse."

Feeling defeated, I collapsed onto my bed, rocking back and forth as I wrote what I believed might be my last will. I stumbled to the bathroom, breaking down completely on the floor, crying out for an end to my pain. As I lay on the grimy tiles, I heard a voice—"Are you alright?" The words echoed through my fog of despair.

This was how I met Mr. Malik. His voice was calm, gentle. He helped me up, his grip steady. "Hold on. Don't give up," he said softly, pulling me up from the bathroom floor and guiding me out of that dark place. I slumped down nearby, still dazed, but his words had somehow broken through the haze.

The next morning, as I sat in the dorm, a woman approached—tall, dressed impeccably in a tailored suit, her deep, curly blonde hair framing intense black eyes that seemed to see straight into my heart. She wore a bracelet on her wrist, similar to the one my lawyer had worn. I felt a sense of dread and relief mingled together. She came close, her voice gentle yet direct.

"Would you like to talk to someone?" she asked. I hesitated, reluctant to let down my guard, and muttered, "I just need an attorney. That's all." She paused and looked at me intently. "Do you feel like hurting yourself?" I swallowed hard, a lump in my throat as I whispered, "I can't do this anymore."

For the first time, someone heard the truth I'd been holding back, and I felt the faintest glimmer of hope, knowing that maybe, just maybe, I wouldn't have to face this darkness alone.

Life on Suicide Watch

The process of being placed on suicide watch took less than five minutes—too fast to truly comprehend what was happening. I noticed an officer stationed near my bed, initially thinking she was just on patrol. But after six hours, I overheard her mutter into her radio, "I am here waiting for the suicide." That's when it hit me: I was on suicide watch.

From that moment, someone came to check on me every four hours, each time asking, "Are you okay?" And each time, I answered, "No! Can anyone be okay in this condition?" But no one ever responded.

After a full 24 hours, a white officer returned and, without explanation, announced, "I am going to take you off suicide watch." Just like that, the "watch" ended. The following day, I heard my name called over the intercom, but I didn't respond. Then it happened again, and again I stayed silent, hoping to detach from the constant surveillance.

Around 7:00 p.m., an officer in a striped white shirt approached me with a microphone. She asked me to confirm my identity by speaking my last name and inmate ID number into it. Frustrated, I complied but couldn't resist adding, "You should already have this information. You're the ones who issued that number to me." Then I told her, "I refuse criminal clinic services, local clinic services, and maternal health social services. I just want to go home." I hoped that by declaring my intentions, they'd understand I wanted no part in the procedural games they were playing.

After a brief pause in activity, things resumed. A woman with a tight wig called my name, asking, "Is that your name?" I answered, "Yes, I'm waiting for you to change it," sarcasm laced in my tone. She shot me a glare that reminded me of the Grinch, but I stared back with equal defiance. I didn't look to the officers for sympathy or favors. If I needed water, I swallowed my saliva. When I ran out of toilet paper, I used my shirt and washed it later. In my first seven days, I managed to survive with just a single bag of toiletries, refusing to let the institution strip away my sense of resilience.

Life on suicide watch wasn't about care or concern; it felt more like another layer of control. Each small act of defiance became a lifeline, a way to keep my identity intact amid the routine deprivation.

Taking Control

For seven days, I managed without access to water, wearing the same clothes for five days before washing them and drying them on the radiator. My routine became my way of asserting independence—I even washed my underwear after each shower, ensuring I could keep going without relying on anyone.

People around me kept mentioning "detox." I ignored it. Drugs had never been part of my life, and I wasn't interested in anyone's assumptions. One day, a counselor came over, suggesting meditation to help with sleep. I replied with a firm "No," making it clear I had no interest in her advice.

With a hint of arrogance, she told me, "Procrastination comes from a lack of self-control." I stared at her, unbothered, and replied, "Counselor, it seems you've forgotten your place. If you're so concerned about my wellbeing, maybe you should speak to my family." Her condescending attitude wasn't something I would let slide.

Just then, the medication officer intervened. "No problem," she said, "I'll take your name off the medication list." I felt an unexpected wave of relief. In that small exchange, I felt as if I was finally reclaiming some agency over my own life. Even within the confines of the jail, I found ways to establish boundaries, reminding myself that I was still in control of who I was and who I intended to be.

Rising Above

I look back on the journey—every challenge, every desperate moment, and every small victory—I realize that the path wasn't just about survival. It was about finding strength I didn't know I had, about resilience in the face of despair, and about creating hope where none seemed to exist.

In those days of darkness, I discovered parts of myself that had been hidden under years of struggle and loss. I found a voice that could speak for others, a heart that could empathize, and a will that refused to be broken. Each setback taught me the power of perseverance, the beauty of connection, and the importance of self-respect, even when it seemed the world had none to offer.

Stepping out of those walls was like stepping into a new life. I had been beaten down, but I had risen. The scars I carry are reminders not of suffering, but of strength and survival. They are a testament to every day I chose to keep going.

Today, I stand on the other side of that struggle with gratitude. I am grateful for the people who, even in the most unexpected places, offered me kindness and support. I am grateful for the family who held me up through it all, and for the strangers who reminded me that humanity exists even in the darkest corners.

But most of all, I am grateful for the strength I found within myself. I now understand that life doesn't always follow a path of fairness or ease, but with determination, courage, and a deep sense of purpose, we can overcome even the harshest of challenges. My story may be filled with pain, but it is equally filled with resilience and redemption.

I move forward, I need to, I do so with a heart that has known both suffering and triumph, with hands that are open to embrace life, and with a spirit that is unbreakable. To anyone facing their own darkness, I say this: *hold on. You are stronger than you know.*

About the Author

My name is Ashney Harryton, and by day, I am a trauma nurse. But I am also a wife, a mother, and a sister. This book is not just about me—it's about the lessons I've learned along the way and the experiences that have shaped who I am. I wrote it to educate, inspire, and enlighten others who might someday find themselves walking a similar path.

This story is my way of ensuring that I leave a mark on this world, not just as a name on a family tree, but as a living, breathing testament to resilience. I want my future generations to know my struggles, my triumphs, and my journey. More importantly, I want others to understand that life is rarely as simple as it seems. Even those who live clean, healthy lives, and follow the law can face unexpected challenges. Bad things can happen to good people, and I hope my story will shed light on that truth.